DELIRIUM
FOR SOLO HARP

For Lisa
A Good Morning
neighbour & friend,
love,
Nadine

DELIRIUM
for Solo Harp

Nadine McInnis

Nadine McInnis

BuschekBooks
Ottawa

Library and Archives Canada Cataloguing in Publication

McInnis, Nadine, 1957-, author
    Delirium for Solo Harp / Nadine McInnis

Poems
ISBN 978-1-894543-84-2 (pbk.)

I. Title

PS8575.I54D44 2015   C811'.54   C2015-901438-7

Illustrations by Nadine McInnis
Cover design by Renée Depocas

Printed in Winnipeg, Manitoba, Canada by Hignell Book Printing

BuschekBooks
P.O. Box 74053
5 Beechwood Avenue
Ottawa, Ontario, Canada K1M 2H9
buschekbooks.com

For Owen,
who speaks the language of music

TABLE OF CONTENTS

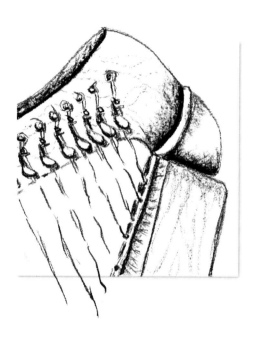

Sing to me of the man, Muse, the man of twists and turns
driven time and time again off course.....

Many pains he suffered, heartsick on the open sea,

Launch out on his story, Muse...
Start from where you will – sing for our time too.

Book One, *The Odyssey*

My pen poised at the first appointment, my questions
laid out, locations and times circled,

ready.

On my lap, an open book –
brown silk cover, a sheaf of empty pages
where hope hovered, waiting to declare itself.

Truer were the stapled sheets
of the hospital's questionnaire,
neatly photocopied:

> On a scale from 1 to 10:
> Is this the worst pain you've ever experienced?
> Rate your nausea, with 0 being no nausea
> and 10 the worst nausea.
> Rate your energy, your mood,
> the support you have at home.

Much more true than the few notes I made:

hemoglobin 90 instead of +130
BP 121 over 69
99% oxygen saturation
ECG?
How often should lithium be checked?

Before my handwriting spins out of control,
trying to keep up with the proliferation of tumours
as the oncologist reads the scan:

> T4 tumour of the colon,
> 9 cm,
> probable liver mets,
> multiple, variably-sized, 3 mm to 3 cm
> nodules, in both lungs and in
> lymph node behind the esophagus,
>
> lesions lining the abdominal cavity.

His heart is fine, kidneys are sluggish
but lungs can take it, the oncologist says to me.
No reason why he can't have surgery.

At last, my father lifts his eyes.

Except that it's spread, he adds matter-of-factly,
and we both exhale.

The silk notebook lies empty from that day on.

·

How shall I sing of a man's twists and turns
as he passes me and vanishes?

Not in notes fixed with ink,

> but with my harp, tuned to mourning.

Alone, facing my own mortality, then his.

In my deep purple room at home,

        remembering,

then in his living room
      so he can hear me from a distance,

finally at his bedside

                accompanying him

when words are lost.

Not notes but a voice
           of many waters and a voice
      of great thunder,

and even things without life can give voice,

      can give distinction

           to his leaving.

Roots

The tree I loved as a child
was blackened by names cut with a knife
before I was born.

The heart that once contained them,

now a spreading bruise,
soon to be indecipherable.

With my ear against this wounded tree,
arms wrapped around the
        forest-cool trunk,

        I knew the loneliness
                of living wood

that did not hug back

        and would cast off my name as well.

ROBIN

The voice is richest just before it breaks,

a luthier told me, cradling
the cherry neck between his big hands.

Stress along the harp's soundboard,
        pressure of thirty-six strings on the pillar,
                is too strong to defy physics forever.

And this harp that I've held humming
between my knees, laid gently
against my shoulder,

is dying now,

the neck, only wood after all,
leaning into its fateful twist.

                •

My father's voice on the phone yesterday
was deep and warm.

The luthier's words were still vibrating
in strings held close to my chest,

        and I felt my heart quiver:

cancer's shadow blooming in his lungs and liver,

        though we did not know it yet.

April was foreshadowing a season of riotous growth,

the quiet before an ugly chord progression,
    the scale eroding,   vertebra by vertebra,
        organs shot through with dull rot.

An organized silence would come soon,
    as viscera gave up his voice.

•

In the night, I wake at 4:00 am, confused,
    as if answering a child's cry.

My father's voice?

A weird light cracks the blinds
    in the living room. The picture-window

        emits snowlight,

    spinning and eddying,

each branch and stone and roof
    lit by radiation,   muffled with white
    against a sooty rust-coloured sky.

Bird song. Strange bird song
has lifted me from my bed,

      a robin

in the branches of the dormant maple.

Scanning, I find the only dark shape
in this world tonight.

How did the bird
shake snow off its shoulders
to sing that way?

Off-time, but dazzling,
mixed up,   but flirting through scales,

breaking chords

delicate ornamental trills ascending,

ascending

even as snow continues to fall.

THREE TRAVELLERS

And where was I when they started their dying?

For my mother, in the Yukon in November,
reading poems she would have hated.
And when I tried to leave, the first blast of winter
iced the ramp to the plane, prevented our departure
as mountains stood rigid, unmoved, invisible
behind the snow-whipped town. Frozen in place
so that I missed my connection and arrived
after the diagnosis, in time for one brief conversation.
We might as well have been at a cocktail party,
So, do you enjoy your job?
I hear you play the harp. Why did you take it up?

For my father, in Italy the next July, haunted in Siena
by his voice in a dream saying, *Goodbye, Nadine.*
so that I called home, shaken by my mother's greeting
still on the answering machine. Travelling on,
to Cinque Terres, five separate worlds swathed in humidity,
I hiked along the terraced vineyards above the sea,
climbed 276 steps in stifling heat to reach
an internet café shadowed within medieval streets.
No response, no response, that silence too eloquent.
My own goodbye to my daughter, spoken in her ear,
as we embraced at the airport: *Don't tell me*
if he dies when I'm gone. was not my last will.
The living can change their minds.

Whichever way I interpret symbols and auguries,
cold so appropriate for her, heat for him,
I was a long way from home.

PLAYING SCRABBLE WITH MY FATHER

These are his words – *weak wilt sorrow soul*

My letters could spell – *death*
attaching to his word – *atheist*

the horizon, a black storm front
we both sense,
                lifting the hair
                        on the back of my neck.

So I hold off, the small room suddenly thick with heat.

The words keep surfacing, kissing the surface
before slipping back down,

                        unbidden, not yet.

His words – *kite   song   witty   plane*
        simple, declarative, words he can make

here and now, where once was

        love   I wait

for this word to surface for him, for me,

it doesn't matter who.

Instead I could piece together – *eulogy*
for 29 glorious points,
                tumbling and bubbling down
                    like a spring from – *soul*

but I am reluctant to pull ahead,

refrain,
>
> turn *eulogy* into *luge*
> reckless twisting down an icy tunnel.

He joins *gene* to *luge*

Are we speaking in riddles?
as his cancer cells slide so efficiently
through his lymph system.

All I have to offer is *never*

a triple letter score, 19:
>
> *never* to slip feet into shoes,
> *never* another snowfall,

nevers are infinite and I withhold again,
> letting him choose the verb.

Each time I walk through the door
of my childhood home and turn

towards his room,
I wonder if morphine has yet stolen

all the words,

if this is the way the game will end.

But he has these last few plays to make,
the letters limited as time

clicking like finger bones
in the night-coloured whiskey sack:

rise

Nothing from me. Then his last silent imperative

go

Cord

Her last word, *No*, only that morning
when I asked her if she was in pain.

The brows her own still, drawn in
to concentrate hard, but not on me.

No, and I sit back, leave her to enter
that nightmare space I can't follow.

Although later, once everyone has gone,
and I'm dozing with her foot in my hand

she'll rush at me with strong pianist's hands
around my neck and I'll rise up gasping

long and harsh as my first breath after the cord
was slipped from my windpipe to my brow

and away, her heartbeat so distant that it might
as well have been silenced, and was, for me

from that moment on.

AEOLIAN

We are blown off course, the chord breaks,
a minor tragedy that touches us most intimately.
Riven, we arrive, our fast small beat

suddenly laden with wind, a cosmic storm
in our lungs, and we breathe.
We do not choose this dark pressure

pushing us down and away, the moan
of our mothers reaching a crescendo as light
slaps us hard, and we gasp with surprise.

Then they are blown off course, hurtling away
from a kitchen full of dishes abandoned
for other hands, the music still open from

when she rose from the piano and never returned,
a season of baseball recorded mindlessly
by the remote. They will not return

to the muddy cliffs of Glace Bay, or
rural crossroads where he trudged through snow
to feed the school's woodstove at dawn,

to shivering water where silver twitches
on its way upstream. The wind chimes I gave
them remain in the maple all winter,

long after she would have lifted them
and carried them inside. They chant
the song of a cold north wind,

keening, swirling. What is outside splits
and rejoins beyond our shelter, where our warm
exhalation clouds the glass.

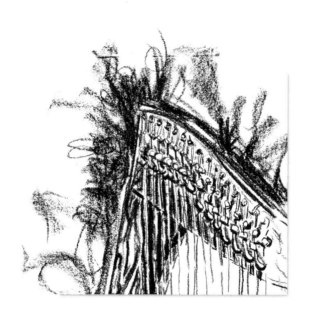

Wood

The harp is both strong and yielding –
    resting on my right shoulder,

sensuous arc leaning over me

      protectively,

the sound is ours alone.

All I knew of harps before
    were frilly glissandos, ornamentation.

I never knew the wood
would warm to my body temperature,

would move as I move,
then stand back, patiently

beautiful   even when silent.

Late afternoon
    slanted light makes the brass strings shine,
      red and blue, C and F frequencies,

    jeweled geometry.

        My hand reaches out,

ribbed strings wound tight as nerves

blurred by my touch

    pulsate
    in the charged air.

My father's dogs

My own dog won't draw near, cries
at the door now, nails scratching to get out,

but his dogs are curled at his head or foot,
a slow sigh
        the only sign of their presence.

Where did that sound come from?

You could never be sure.

My footfall does not disturb their sleep.

Never in the flesh, yet the dogs are here,

What day is it?
Do you remember that time we....?

I shift one photo after another to remind him.

Often, he looks at me blankly, unable to recall,
        but when he calls out, alone in his dim room

these ones come running:

        Pilot. Mac. Buddy.

And the stories come when they are called too,
bright light streaking towards us,

even if fragmented,

                    prismatic,

          lives reawakened.

A haphazard fishing trip, his footing lost,
Mac grabbing his collar,
               towing him with sharp teeth to the bank.

He actually laughs at a Christmas cake
devoured by Buddy,
                    wrapping paper and all,

                         and later,
               red and green festooning the snow.

These ones are cumulus drifting across the floor,

                              a wild leap
through a screen door,

                    and they're free.

He describes deaths, too, suddenly lucid.

His wavering voice, barely audible,
tells me how old, how hard,

               how much he cried
when they were shot, as farm dogs always were,
never held gently as they left.

I am the ghost here:

I'm just going to wash your face and hands.
Do you want anything to drink?
Is your mouth dry?

He does not answer. There is no need.

Muzzles, soft and warm, prod him,
reposition him when he lies too long in one place.
Sleek heads slip under his feverish hands.

He knows whose moist breath
                                        moves along his arms,

whose gentle tongue washes his face clean.

Steel strings

Unwind the dull brass,

    and the harp curves naked,

        vulnerable until

shiny steel glitters in the lower register.

The ends of strings wound me,
    piercing my finger pads,

    sharp talons I thread through
    tuning pegs,

winding tight, painfully taut.

The harp wounds me – I wound the harp.
I cry out,

    the harp cries back.

STINGS

When will the hypodermics begin, I brood on a break
with my dog, who whines to escape the sick house,
as I once did, yanking against the short leash of adolescence.

By habit, my feet lead me to scrub land, the power line,
a rare rough passage of brambles and yearnings
owned by no one, so I don't notice their young voices.

Ma'am, the boys call to me from the thorn bushes,
Stay away, Ma'am, warning me away from the frizzled
base of a hydro tower where black thorns click.

The power lines above us sizzle and buzz.
My dog knows enough to heed the boys' advice,
senses that one boy holds a stick, but not for chasing,

and herds me gently towards the edge of the field.
Or does he anticipate peppery wings, black and mean?
A hornet's nest knocked down, summer coming to an end.

Next week these boys will long for corridors of wildness
so why not beat the end of freedom with a stick?
Not knowing, why should they, that my father

is their future as well as mine. School and the end
of summer are temporary setbacks as they race
towards the ransacked hub lying on its side,

grey as death, crushed, the papery layers evacuated.
The nest is finished and there's only hell to pay.
Swarming hate homes in on them, reckless.

Stung, one boy screams and it's hilarious to them both.
Lady, you better keep clear of here, lady,
they screech as they dance on hot coals and taunt

all of history's pestilence to pursue them. Not knowing
that stings find you anyway, careful or not,
even when a person is as old as I must seem.

Neck

The lighter the wood,
          airier the tone.

Some wood is too knotted
          to be sliced into thin
               wafers of voice.

Cherry is best,
          stained red grain,

warm as a pulse when played in the sun.

And sweet, so sweet.

Sitka spruce sheared to the nerves
unfurled around the
          umbilical knots that hold strings tight.

          So sensitive I shivered
             the first time

          my hand brushed its curves.

Now I covet the darkest wood,
          hardest heart of dark walnut,

          density a weight pushing me down,

          voice of coffee,   chocolate,
             dark storm clouds,
               sultry afternoons.

Jo M'enamori d'un aire

Illicit, the way

he hides his hands
when I notice the tremor.

He's still in bed at noon
but tells me he's already had breakfast,

he eats the cake I made
for his final birthday

but quietly slips away to throw up.
He has a dusting of my mother's ashes

on his fingertips even though he says
he's over his grief.

The sheets on his bed are a dank tangle,
a puzzle to revisit charged with emotion.

I fell in love with fragrance
the fragrance of a young man.

He says, *I don't know what to say,*
when I ask him if he wants me to leave.

His delirium is all kindness,
he's a gentleman offering burnt potatoes

from under his bed. His animal instinct
makes him hide his weakness.

I think of his body whenever
I'm away in my own bed at night.

I fell in love by night,
to the moonlight I was prey.

I notice the shape of his pelvis,
the bone structure of a young man

quickly revealed through his last summer,
the way I'm troubled at 3:00 am

woken from a dream – I'm lying beside him
feeling the pain he won't express.

If ever again I fall in love
let it be by the clear light of day.

We retreat to his dark bedroom
for the last days, curtains closed

against the sun. The way I can read his mind:
You've always hated this time of year.

Me too, and although he's not strong enough
to nod, I feel him nod.

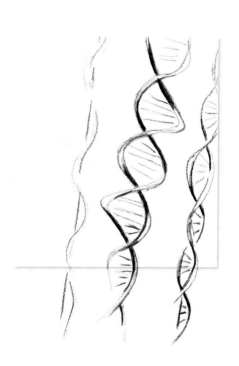

Gut strings

A tallowy smell close to the nose.

Intimate to fingertips, cheek,
my head bent low to catch the warm

        whiff of body, yellowish old bones
            sticky in summer heat.

At the science museum the living line up for hours
        to gain entry to *Body Worlds*,

                and what do I find but my harp

                        deconstructed.

Human bodies   plasticized,   dissected,
        skin peeled back to reveal
                  muscles,

tendons and ligaments. I could pluck,
sitting on my little stool,

            and draw this dissected man
to me.

Muscles are shades
        of teak, walnut-hued liver, cherry-wood heart.

The man in my harp –
the harp in every man.

But my harp's voice is only

    a reverberation

of what was once alive.

I love you, he said to the nurse
  he mistook for me.

She told me this when he was sleeping

    and all my life I've only ever heard this echo
of his voice in hers.

Not even waving, just drowning

No goodbyes from mom, no phone
wanted in her room. My dad had not been
well enough to drive her, so a neighbor did
what neighbours do, brought her to the hospital.
My mother coughed up blood, but we only knew later
after she died and I stripped her bed, these little
November roses on her pillowcase, every rent
in tissue evicting her with less than a week's notice.

No requests for visits, the youngest grandchild
took too much energy, my father oblivious
to her fate, no long lost daughter requested
to reconcile with now that time was short, no advice,
no grown grandchildren summoned a last time.
She'd done this before alone, given birth
on those distant sanitary wards astringent with bleach,
masked, her head lolling to the hiss of the gas canister
and was glad to be done with that too.

Although we did come the last day she could speak,
gowned and gloved to spare her our pathogens.
Your eyes are alike, she said, looking at me, at my
grown daughter. *Just like yours,* I said. *That's genetics.*
I was naked behind my drapings and mask, my eyes filling,
my sadness the only part visible, the naked eye.

WATER SPIRIT

Oh, to be so thirsty as this hummingbird
sipping again and again at the red balloon
in the neighbour's yard wavering in the riffling breeze
shrunken now to the size of a withered plum.

No flower, even though the balloon twists on its slender string,
No time to waste. The hummingbird's heart
beats so fast it cannot sleep and its thimble-full
of blood craves simple sugars.

Then holding the red straw to his pale lips
that tremble, I watch the spirit level of cranberry juice
rise and fall, rise and fall, his hard labour
before he receives a faint moistening of false comfort.

Spirits

Before he became a spirit
he gave up spirits for good.

I left out berries he would not touch,
then glasses beaded with fresh cold.

The way the scooped glacier of a blue salt lick
pulls winter-burned deer out of the forest,

or scraped mink skins pull the wolf,
or the glittering line of sugar lures the ants,

this is how the living trap the living
before dispatching them to death.

But my heart was pure, and he was distilling,
a strange vapour lifting from his open mouth.

Here is apple, here is grape, but nothing tempts him,
try pomegranate cut with sparkling water

then cocktail mixtures, elixirs he sniffed,
Is this alcoholic? before turning away.

Who would have guessed he would doubt
after chasing spirits all the years of my youth?

He promised me proof, even as he turned away.
In a dream, by some arcane system of symbols.

Now, as at his bedside, I sit, continuous still
as he cools and falls as night dew.

Delirium

Comings and goings of all of us, lost keys and guests
and food that's spoiled and the goat is upside down
above the roof and he can't find his keys
and has to be somewhere, away from this prison.
He doesn't know why he's in jail, the legs of the side
table on either side of his head after he falls out of bed.
They don't come, but you have the key, don't you?
Don't leave without him, he has money in his wallet
to pay you. *Can you spirit me away?* he asks,
breaking your heart as you lift his bones from the floor.

Comings and goings, they had their ways of leaving.

Simple enough for her through the piano, moonlight dappling
my Saturday morning bed, *Pathetique sonata*, the sad passion
of my mother alone in the living room, washes of empathy and stunning
courage, savage heart bared through her hands' strength,
pulling her own ribcage open, beating heart of her rhythms,
the blurred roar of the piano bass shaking the moonlight
on my bed into ripples, and then I woke to sunlight,
the notes assuming their ancient patterns, repeated
as long as people still care to play them. Not forever,
but long enough for her.

Rhythm

I can count the beat, finger marking air,
foot tapping inside my shoe,
or voice it when alone.

I can calculate, use reason, mark the place
where silence breaks with faint lead on paper

but rhythm will not live until I feel it.

When he is conscious, I do not touch him.
When he is well enough

we talk, his breath a steady easy whoosh
under the stories that come fast, one after another,
bursting with physical energy,

the way his heart will speed up, manic, in the hours
just before his death.

*Bend down, hold your breath, empty pickle vats 12 hours a day
in the Leamington Heinz factory, worst job I ever had, but it
was always available. Spiking on the railway gang, then I was
a bolter upper for building mine sweepers during world war
two, Trenton car works, tobacco picker, I got my first job at 8 in
the one room school house, made the fire in the box stove before
dawn, brought my kindling, paid $5 for the whole year. After
the war I travelled for the petition to sign for lights, some people
wanted to keep their oil lamps, kerosene. I was working in the
lumber camp when I wrote the provincials, that year I was the
only one to pass. My fishing record was over 100 trout, my dad
was thrilled, I cast out once, so far I couldn't see and then the
line unreeled completely, pulled taut and I yanked and wrestled*

with all my strength, the whole rod took off into the sky and a
duck flew above the trees leaving me cursing...

Then the metronome's tick grows louder
and all I can hear are his breaths, one by one,
breaking the silence that stole his words.

I touch him, just the wrist, where the pulse
twitches impatiently,
press my fingers below the useless watch
I'm too sad to remove.

Fhear a 'Bhata

How often haunting the highest hilltop
I scan the ocean, a sail to see.

His ribcage is the shape of a hollow whelk,
blades of calcium arc over salt sludge
drying to sifted stars at the back of his spine.

His hands curled in the hollow, sheltering,
homeless beneath the girders
of a cold bridge.
Never to reach or hold anything again.

His hands rest under the shipwreck of his ribs,
too heavy to search pockets the dead never have
arriving or leaving.

Will it come tonight, will it come tomorrow?

If I put my ear to his chest
would I hear the sea?

Leaning in, I could gather his ribs against my ribs,
the solid bone of his sternum and shoulders,
so stable they will weigh a stone
even as ash.

Will it ever come to comfort me?

His ribs press, tense as strings,
and I understand the ancient shape of the lyre:
strong shoulders, a slender waist,
tendons and strings.

Farewell, wherever you be,

nerves of this narration,
plucked and known by heart.

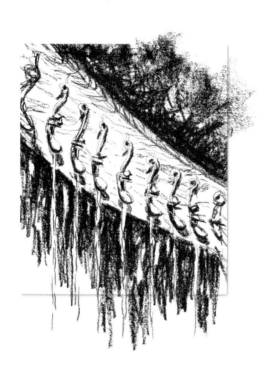

LEVERS

Who will leave whom?   A harp
has limitations.

Mastered by physics,
the levers lift his voice a semi-tone,

no more.

Tuning pegs slip a little in the night,

his voice slipping further away.

Wrench of my wrist pulls him back,

but harps age faster than people do.

At thirty years
his life will be over.

My hands were taught to close gently
with each pluck,

like holding a butterfly
without damaging the wings.

Open   I release
and they drift to settle on the next strings.

As a child   I caught rusty moths by the wings,
my fingerprints slick black
where the powder blotted away,

and moths climbed onto my hand without flying away.

What a fool I was,

believing they wanted nothing
more than to touch me

with their wounded wings.

Thirty years ago, I met my husband.

Thirty years from now, the butterflies in my hands

will be crushed,

I'll scratch at the harp and he'll refuse to hold

his tune. A hairline fracture
will grow between us
and in that fine black line,

silence will take root.

LETTING GO

He won't let go:

Moved his car through a car wash once,
in drive instead of neutral, banging and racing
through the storm, felt strips whipping the windshield,
dryer bouncing off the hood of the car,
Your car wash is broken, he complained.
You should get it fixed.

The price for a second run, the attendant's laughter.

Or right hand locked on the lever in the cafeteria,
one glass bowl of ice cream became two as he grabbed another,
then another, and another, five in all,
before my mother broke the current
by grabbing his arm. *Just let go*, she screamed at him.

I know that anger. He was in my house once
when I didn't want him near me for years,
walked right through the unlocked door when I was ill
from grief at how he'd failed me.
Get out, I told him. *Get off my couch.*
He slowly lifted his eyes: *I'm still your father.*
Heart pounding, listening
for his steps from the basement. I never saw him leave.

Couldn't let go of the new snow blower either,
the sight of green confetti thrown in the white air
brought us to the door. He was being dragged
on his back along the edge of the driveway
as the blades chewed up the cedar hedge.
Let go and it stops! we yelled in unison but he couldn't.

He couldn't take the anesthetic for the shock treatments
either, fought losing consciousness every time,
hated that rapid plunge into sleep even more
than the current passing through his brain.

What is this current that locks him into life.
Four suicide attempts not enough to break its hold?
I want to be asleep when it happens, he tells me
with a dubious expression. And I lie to him:
You probably will be. Most people are.

So this is what I say to him between songs,
when he's past words of his own:

> We're all fine. You've left us well taken care of. We're
> grown. You saw Mom through and she never had to
> be alone. Your parents have gone too. We'll be along in
> a while, not too soon, but in a while. We'll remember
> you as a character. Your grandchildren will tell their
> grandchildren crazy stories about you. I remember
> the blue jacket your mother knit for you.

> *An anchor,* his last words.

Yes, I forgot that white anchor in the pattern. You were
a good father, always happy to see us. The rest doesn't
matter, only that. You survived that awful illness.
Bipolar didn't get you. What an accomplishment!
You're not dead, yet.

> An exhalation that could be a laugh. I hope it's a laugh.

Last month I was in Catherine of Siena's house and saw a fresco of her first miracle, floating up the stairs when she was 8 years old. I dreamt of you last night. You drifted down the stairs just like St. Catherine, in your new blue pyjamas and silently appeared in the family room where we were and I helped you into your chair. You weren't speaking. Like you were in the afterlife, but still with us.

I don't say, *let go, let, go, you can go,* but instead:

You're stuck in this old carcass, aren't you?

And his mouth twitches up on one side,

his last smile.

ARRAN BOAT SONG

Put off, put off, and row with speed,
for now is the time and the hour of need.

I play an old song of swift escape,
leaning in close to the bed.

His breathing tidal, deeper, then shallower,
pauses, and I play on.

Sun glows on curtains closed against what remains
of summer, and I breathe in this deeper pause.

We steer by the light of the taper's gleam.

I keep watching the sweet blurred strings.

His breathing tidal, deeper, then shallower,
a caesura, and I play more.

Stay calm, play on, to oars, to oars
and pluck the notes from the air,
give him this accompaniment, this privacy,

chime sweetly to the dashing shore.

His breathing tidal, deeper, then shallower,
a pause, and I play near.

These ponderous keys shall the kelpies keep
and lodge in their caverns dark and deep.

Put off, put off, and row with speed
for now is the time and the hour of need.

Dream Habanera

The rhythm changed, a breathless catch
a broken wing dragged in gravel,

then a flutter, a flap of breath,
swooning, but still held aloft.

I stood from my harp and moved
to his folded wing, attentive,

holding my own breath,
the piercing quills of silence soon

dropped, with the useless rising
and falling in his hollow throat.

Through strength of will or reflex,
he pulled breath into him again.

I touched his shoulder as three breaths
came easily, then a rough exhalation

and more attempts to breathe.
It's OK Dad, I said. He breathed again,

that swooping lurching dance
between parent and child.

I could hear again my daughter's
first stumbling breaths, the suctioning,

my own breath held as I rode the updrafts
above the red canyon still pulsing

from the surgeon's scalpel, a slow dip
into animation, then she arrives

as he leaves, a tear released from
beneath the right eyelid.

Reflex or emotion? *He heard you,*
the nurse says and my hand hovers

but he does not reach out and take it,
the dance between us abandoned.

My daughter bends with the stethoscope,
listens at chest and throat,

and I open my hand, need to hear the silence
too. A rubber tube slithers down my chest

cool, almost wet, like the cord that joined
me to my mother and her to me.

Under a silver dome: dense silence
where once there was rhythm,

static scratchy and magnified on the surface
of his flesh, only the rough friction of matter.

Voyage

He undertakes this last voyage alone.
I've held his cooling hand,
slipped his watch, still warm and moist
from the dry husk of his arm,
his gold ring is hard as a pebble against
my palm. I'm waiting to hurl it,
watch the echoes move out and dissipate
but not yet. I've rocked and closed,
my forearms pressed against my clenched
and guarded viscera. Let him go still
wearing the pyjama top cut up the back
with scissors. Let his ribcage go, already
hollowed but not hungry. Let his feet go
without a need for shoes. The Scottish hook
of his nose stands down as sentry
and I withdraw as well, leaving my harp
to witness his levitation from the bed,
his floating, feet first, down the stairs.
So silently he is lifted, silent as the strings
stiffening and giving up all echo of my hands,
not even the front door can be heard
opening, then closing.

Reversal

She is spared his death
ten months after her own.

After four attempts to die, after scrawled notes
I never saw, after her being questioned by the police,

after his prostate cancer, blood poisoning,
having to learn how to flush the tubes,

after adrenaline shocks to the stunned heart,

how strange that he should be at her hospital bed
just hours before her death,

his hand a little too harsh, too weighted
on her forehead, and she unable to resist

when he says, *I think she likes it,*
meaning his clumsy stroking that lifts her brows.

In his shock and confusion thinking that if
his children are all here, this is a party of sorts.

Her rapid death, only on this day forming bruises,
a dark map of continents spiriting her away.

CLAIMING THE BODY

My father didn't want to see her again.
My brother didn't want to see her
after the hospital morgue gave her up.
I didn't need to see her,
having been with her when she died,
but the funeral home wanted us to see her
to confirm that the ashes would be hers.

In this case, the ID can be waived,
he said, looking at me
because the family resemblance is so strong,

and I shivered.

Not her, not my mother, but death claiming me.

Later he handed me an unmarked envelope
containing her wedding rings,
the ones I tried and failed to slip from her fingers
with soap her last night in the hospital,
expecting them to be cut and twisted open
but they fell into my palm
two perfect circles of gold

from her disarticulated hands.

LAST RITES

We didn't arrange any memorial to him,
so exhausted from his hard death.
Nothing to balance our elaborate ceremony for her,
the priest saying her name over and over
and caressing holy water onto the urn,
the performance of each of her children
and grandchildren, live music, classical, jazz,
original composition, a wind quintet, harp,
a poem read, only a touch ironic,
mummy, about Egyptian passage to the underworld
and my dad so proud, *I gave all my talent away*, he said.

Do I regret the cards that didn't get mailed,
the green garbage bag in his room receiving his socks,
cufflinks, smudged reading glasses.
Do I regret watching a surfing documentary
a few hours after his body left?
No, but I regret not taking the time
to dress him better before he was carried away.
He went in his ugly beige pyjamas top cut roughly up the back
by the nurse's scissors and a diaper he didn't need.

I took the watch, still warm and humid from his wrist,
the Saint Frances Xavier ring with its black cross on gold
from his hand, but I should have dressed him
in his favourite shiny shirt and cowboy tie, the turquoise
stone jaunty, a good leather belt, dress shoes.

What did I fear? The rough tussle on his bed
a little unsavory, even with him still so pliable
and beyond sensation? Did I fear laying my length along his length,
reaching into his drying dislocated mouth to place
the dentures I threw out that afternoon back into place?
Seeing his smile again?

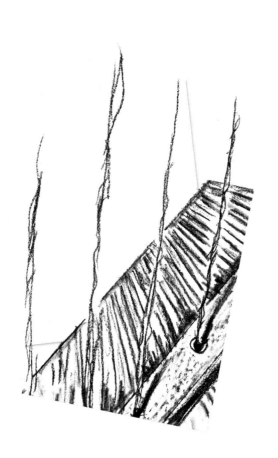

Sounding board

I met him in a forest,
        although I didn't recognize it yet.

Oh, the echo
                the first time I touched a harp.

Electric response,   wires and gut carrying a current

        splitting wind,
                        slashing the red heart,   setting sun
                        in winter.

Voice trying to get through
        and here it is   unscrambled at last

                making perfect sense.

I lean in, tell him
                I'm afraid of getting old, of dying alone.

The harp murmurs,

A voice is most beautiful just before

                it dies. If you were a harp,
                you would know this.

My head low, I whisper,

        almost kissing
                        the sounding board,

confessing.

His response   so soft   no one else could hear:

Resonance is all there is –

      touch

                sends wood and strings into waves,

cycles of vibration.

      Waves move beyond,   so much larger
      than the small gesture,
                    small contraction

      of a forefinger.

BREATH

The tide turns
rattling detritus, weeds
and bones, stones and shells,
a loud drag of pebbles
across the ocean floor,
then a windy push,
a soft moist roar, before a quiet
pause that lets sound build again.

Uneven, like the breath of the dying
or the muscle contractions,
practicing birth, the belly hard
as tumours, hard as a reminder
of just how hard it is
to leave the body
in the beginning and at the end,
no difference.

Into my mother's body
they pushed platelets and blood,
oxygen and antibiotics,
but nothing could seed her with life.
The tide turned,
she breathed and coughed,
turned blue whenever they
cleaned her mouth of thick
secretions, corrosive as salt,
her lungs stagnant, breath
barely circling.

She was drowning
when the tide turned
as she'd always feared.

She was pulled out
by morphine, her breathing
forced, she was dragged
rattling and clanking
like a chain over the rough
stones below,

and when the anchor caught,
she stopped bobbing for breath.

Sea birds cried and circled, bruising her face
with their shadows.

MIRRORS

Their bedroom always had one, rectangular and wide,
silvered, screwed solidly into the back of the dresser,
with my grandmother's hand mirror from the 1920s
facing downwards on the cluttered surface.

After he is gone, I watch myself sweeping away the
storm debris, the mouth swabs and bed pads, the pile
of loose change he dumped from his pockets
when he still needed pockets.

Trying not to, I catch myself in that mirror
eyes sunken with fatigue, so much older. Trapped
instead of willing, I've lost all desire to lift
my grandmother's mirror, turn my back, and glimpse

infinity swooping away in its green depths. So infinite
is this emptiness I feel. No warm breath upon the mirror,
no more catching him unaware, hip to throat,
in bright light, in low lamplight, shadow of him there again.

Decades of his reflection walked in and out the door
to hallway, to bathroom, how many times?
And then he falls and cannot rise to his feet again.
The mirror abandons him a week before he is gone,

catches only his tired children carrying futile drinks
with bendy straws, wet washcloths, then the stranger
filling her hypodermic in daylight, by lamplight, a dim echo
of her quiet movement bringing him brief glimpses of relief.

Ashes

He didn't fit, couldn't be squeezed into the urn,
a film of plastic between my mother's ashes
and his own.

What do you want me to do? the undertaker asked
and not being able to stand the thought of his body
divided, a finger here, a spine there,
I said, *Mix them together, if that will make him fit,*

unaware how he would weigh her down.

Her ashes, ivory and light as powder, bone fragments
glittering like clean sand. Carrying the urn in, she was one armful
balanced on my hip, so lightly she left.

So heavily he arrived, the urn must be heft with bent knees,
an anchor catching on to the living,
a stone in a field impossible to pry loose, stuffed to the lid
with chunks of grey, sharp flinty bones,
rough basalt, reluctant to rest easily.

THERE IS A WHIRLPOOL

I cannot sing but
I can pluck, the sound an ancient
offshoot of war or hunger.

I tell you this that you may see into your hearts.

Fifteen thousand years ago, blood-tinged
paint captured the hunt, the bow straining,
gut string pulled close to the heart,
the velocity of the arrow shot straight to the future
pierces me where I'm vital.

Do not seek to know what forces move you.

Five thousand years ago the bard was buried
in a Pharaoh's tomb.
Sealed in with stone, anointed
with perfumed oil, he sang of battles
and bravery and wisdom in a language
the slaves did not understand

but I understand.

A place where voices echo,
where voices encircle and woo you
as if calling within a cave.

And heard first in mid-life
beneath the snapping gutteral Gaelic,
a voice in the fire as cold pressed my back,

beneath the chanting of medieval monks,
the mosquitoes in the cedars at dusk,

beneath the water skaters who open their hands
to ride high upon ripples of the lake,

*where words grow slow and clear
as the watery depths.*

Caught in the cage of my DNA spiraling
back through my father's line,
that clan of archers served a more powerful clan.

Through my mother's passion,
with her full belly pressed against piano keys,
her music far off as a fog horn, summoning me,
warning me, before language or consciousness,
her music competing with the sound
of her heartbeat and breathing.

There is life and death, both immutable.

These strings came to me,
memory made flesh.

The rest is mere words.

Nurses

The last seven days of my father's undoing
the nurses came with their industry,
their props and pillows and potions.
His dislocation would be complete with
or without their help.
All would recede, fall into the void
from which it came, but the nurses were here
and even I saw that it was good.

One calmed the animal wildness of his pain
with a wasp's sting, the sharp piercing of flesh
that wouldn't exist a week from now.
She plotted the course he followed at he rushed away,
rehearsed what can only be done once
and for all.

One swept back the curtains in the morning,
turned him towards the light,
while another reversed the pattern 12 hours later,
glassy clink of rings sliding along a rail,
positioned him with back turned
to the cooling darkness of summer's end.
Back and forth, all the nurses' agency, their own
clear division of day from night.

One wanted dominion over the linen closet,
removed and refolded sheets, organized them
according to colour and pattern
so that sheets I hadn't seen since the '70s
were suddenly at the front, wild daisies,
psychedelic splashes of rose and violet
cleanly intersected by stripes.

One lifted heavily onto her feet, brought food
into the room that was no longer his own but
a kind of nursery, long after his appetite was obsolete,
consuming her own offerings to shore up her strength
against the terrible weight of all she knows.
The day you become one who eats, you must surely die.

One sat with him through the night,
streetlight catching a glimmer of her right eye,
the bony carapace of her brow,
her full lips just the idea of shape,
the blackness of her skin just a form
for the pale shape of her nylon scrubs, rasp of a ghost
re-crossing its legs.

And the last one arrived for her shift a day after his death,
a bird blown off course, the bed already stripped,
and she sat at the dining room table apologizing,
then took flight as soon as possible,
leaving her raincoat behind. The coat folded its dark wings,
waited on a hook for the weather to turn,
and months later, rain became snow.

In the Bleak Midwinter

They are not gone although they are dead.
Earth stood hard as iron,
water like a stone.
Snow had fallen, snow on snow,
snow on snow.

In the bleak midwinter, I dream
of them dying again, breath on breath,
hard as iron, dry mouth parched,
oh heaven cannot hold them
nor earth sustain.

In the bleak midwinter
I make him die four nights,
the morphine mean, thready pulse,
his breath almond sweet,

riffling across my sleeping brow.
Must he barely live like this?
heaven and earth shall flee away
but he remains.

Four times in life, I lived his death,
rehearsed my grief. For most of us
the hearse only arrives once,
but he chose poison not strong enough
to overcome his animal will to live:
on the garage floor in October,
in the car on the driveway
his locked office in February,
finally the living room at 5 am.

Snow had fallen, snow on snow,
snow on snow in the bleak midwinter
long ago. The hospital, a stable place,
sufficed to allow his death at home,

and this last death
the dream daughter can't escape.
Could you hear me? Was dying terrible?

Yes, and then it went blank. Not too bad.

Oh heaven cannot hold him
nor earth sustain.

What can I give them,
poor as I am? A lamb for the slaughter
instead of suffering? Entrails to untangle
the coils of kinship. If I were wise
I'd find my part, and give what I can,

offer up my beating heart.

Thugamar fein an Samhradh linn

He never got the summer he wished for

all winter: the ease of barbeque for his appetite,
riffling of the backyard umbrella in a warm breeze,

sitting contentedly on the front porch
even though my mother's chair was empty.

I'll be over it by then, he said, meaning her death,
so certain he would be alright on his own.

If the perennials unfurled, if the wind chimes gently
collided, if he could get to the lake in Nova Scotia
where he fished for trout as a boy.

Instead, there were curtains drawn against the sun,
rails installed on his bed, mouth swabs
and endurance for what was left to him of life.

And I endured too, counting the days of the week,
weeks in the month. He'll be gone by the first cool nights,

he'll be gone before morning fog, long before
the last cricket, raspy voice of wind in dead grass.

And he was. On the last Sunday I was sleeveless,

he went.

So here is summer coming for you,
even if nine months too late:

Summer, summer milk from the calves.
We brought the summer with us.

Rain sips from the clouds, winter-packed soil
opens its creaky hinge and swallows
as swallows swoop, scooping life from the drenched air.

Eavestroughs tumbling with tree pollen,
shimmering sound, the faint fire of frog song.

Holly and hazel and elder and rowan.
We brought the summer with us.

Winter crows are chased away by the hawk's appetite,
swift as the fox on its midnight rounds,
tree tops humming with fresh green.

We brought the summer with us.
And bright ash-tree at the mouth of the ford.

Blind tunneling moles burst into bright light.
A warm breeze tosses hatchlings into the air.

Summery greenery, we brought the branch with us.
We brought the summer with us.

This is the moment. This is our time.

We brought the summer with us.
We brought it with us, and who'd take it from us?
We brought the summer with us.

Branches reach with still-small leaves
creased and unique, fresh as fingerprints,
sticky green on our skins. We are touched into life.

MOTHER'S DAY

Is the way I'm alone here with the ocean,
calmed, content in my solitude,
my grown children on other coastlines,
the same way my mother was happy
alone with music? How little she needed
any of us.

The riffling little waves moving fast
towards shore, are light as her hands,
fingers over thumbs, cresting
near middle C,

and the smell of her exertions
is the clean sweat smell of the tide line,
a white quake of sound
that suddenly overtakes the shore.

A piece of bird skull,
sinuous eye holes empty of any small tragedy,
delicate and white as my mother's
bone china, arrives at my feet,
wrapped in seaweed, the ribbons undone
by waves.

With the sound of breathing, of soft
crescendos, the way the waves
give a strong push, then retreat,
she's sent me this on mother's day.

Summer, 1924

If there is an afterlife, you'll be hearing from me,
my father said during his last summer.

I wouldn't mind at all, I answered without pause
and maybe that's why I'm happy he's found me
on this island he never visited.

The summer after his death, there is his profile -
mouth slack, nose hooked, a swaying shadow
on the wall of the little house overlooking Seal Cove
that I bought with his money.

I know it's him, and not a hydrangea tree
shaken in moonlight. He's come to me as well
in a photograph of a frozen puddle of dead leaves
taken on a winter hike to Spring Rock,
leaning into a wind so fierce it dried salt
to white crystals itching on my cheeks.
His death mask, plain to see.
Oh, that's too creepy, my son says
and turns away.

But I don't mind any form he takes.

I'm here where twice a day I can walk
on the ocean's floor, leave my footprints
temporarily on rippled sand far from shore.

I am alone, and he sends a Google alert, first in 3 years
from the site: *Find a grave*, and there is my name,
married to his name, both of us long gone,
since 1924, buried in Scranton, Pennsylvania.

Is this his gallows humour, true to his last word,
or a final piece of fatherly advice?
Latin scholar that he was, I think: *carpe diem.*

He may be the reason I sense the other ghosts
in this house too, the young couple who
built it in 1924, the summer of my father's birth.

The man's young strong back sweating as he sawed
the beams by hand, her keenness for their lives to begin,
scrubbing the new herringbone hardwood as he nailed
Douglas fir bracing to keep the ceiling in place, a cross-hatching
that's held the stars in its net every night since.

She gave birth twice and died too soon in my room
with the tall window overlooking the sea,
yet I sleep easily here.

Today I found her grave tucked under a spruce tree.
Gone at 29, my daughter's age, buried apart
from her young husband, who filled a lifetime after her
and lies now in a different cemetery
beside another, more durable, wife.

But her essence surfaces, especially in the evening,
like a small porpoise arcing dark through silver,
briefly shining in slanted sun before sliding beneath again.

I know the certain sheen of her smooth skin,
the laughing way she stokes the fire, the way
on summer nights, she listens just as I do
to pebbles shift as the tide goes out, her hands
under the quilt feeling the baby move.
This living woman, her name so perfect: Joy.

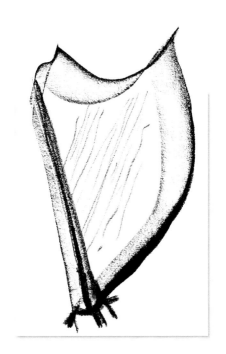

Sources

Quotation from *The Odyssey* is from the translation by Robert Fagles.

Suite of harp music for poems by the same name:

Robin is a slow melancholy 16th century dance written by John Munday. Deborah Friou arranged a beautiful version in her book *Renaissance Music for the Harp*.

Aeolian is part of a suite for Celtic harp written by Owen Fairbairn. The title refers to a particular mode, a system of chords and scales, originally developed in ancient Greece.

Je M'enamori d'un aire is an old Sephardic folksong by an unknown writer in which a woman bemoans falling in love with the wrong man by moonlight.

Water Spirit was written and recorded by the American harpist Kim Robertson.

Fhear a 'Bhata is an old Gaelic song often performed on the Celtic harp.

Arran Boat Song is an old Gaelic song that tells the story of the escape by sea of Queen Mary from certain death at the hands of British military.

Dream Habanera, written with the rhythm of a slow Cuban tango-like dance, is a beautiful solo harp piece written and recorded by the Canadian harpist Sharlene Wallace.

Voyage is an instrumental harp piece written by Canadian harpist (and my teacher) Lucile Brais Hildeshiem and is the title piece for her most recent CD.

There is a Whirlpool is arranged by the Spanish harpist Arianna Savall and is based on a poem by the Catalan poet Miquel Marti i Pol (translated by Jacqueline Minett).

In the Bleak Midwinter is a poem by Christina Rossetti, which has been turned into a hymn by Gustav Holst, often sung by choirs at Christmas. A lovely harp version can be found arranged by Sunita Staneslow in the harp collection *Christmas Eve*.

Thugamar féin an Samhradh linn, is an old Celtic tune associated with ceremonies celebrating the coming of summer.

Acknowledgements

Some of these poems were published in *Arc* and in the *Saint John Telegraph*. I thank the Ontario Arts Council and the City of Ottawa for grants that gave me the gift of time. Thanks as well to the little house in Seal Cove, Grand Manan, where many of these poems were written and all the illustrations were born.

Thanks to Andrée Christensen, Sandra Nicholls, Ian Roy, Rhonda Douglas, Marsha Barber, Deanna Young, and Moira Farr, who read the manuscript with sensitivity, while giving me some needed objectivity. Thanks as well to my husband, Tim Fairbairn and children Nadia Fairbairn and Owen Fairbairn, for their suggestions and perceptions of both the poems and that summer of my father's decline. I am grateful to designer Renée Depocas for weaving all the disparate visual elements into a seamless whole.

My parents, Corrine Connor McInnis (born in Glace Bay, Nova Scotia on October 23, 1925, died November 5, 2008) and Charles Everett McInnis (born in Antigonish, Nova Scotia on July 12, 1924, died September 13, 2009), endured their deaths with more grace than I ever would have imagined. These poems are testimony to that grace.

The drawings depict details of my 36-string walnut harp made by Timothy Harps, Annapolis, Nova Scotia. The cherry harp with the fatal flaw was also a Timothy harp that has not yet broken and still has a beautiful voice. *Aeolian* was written on this harp.

Author

Nadine McInnis is the author of eight previous books of poetry, short fiction and literary criticism. She is a past winner of the Ottawa Book Award and CBC Literary Competition. Her last book, *Blood Secrets* (short stories, Biblioasis), was long-listed for the international Frank O'Connor Short Story Award and short-listed for the Ottawa Book Award. Her last book of poems, *Two Hemispheres* (Brick Books), was short-listed for the ReLit Award, the Lampman-Scott Award and the Pat Lowther Award. She is a professor at Algonquin College in Ottawa, teaching in the Professional Writing program.